OUR UNIVERSE

Mars

BY MARION DANE BAUER
ILLUSTRATED BY JOHN WALLACE

Ready-to-Read

Simon Spotlight
New York London Toronto Sydney New Delhi

For my grandson, Brannon Bauer, with love — M. D. B.

To Simon and Betsy — J. G. W.

SIMON SPOTLIGHT
An imprint of Simon & Schuster Children's Publishing Division
1230 Avenue of the Americas, New York, New York 10020
This Simon Spotlight edition August 2021
Text copyright © 2021 by Marion Dane Bauer
Illustrations copyright © 2021 by John Wallace
SIMON SPOTLIGHT, READY-TO-READ, and colophon are registered
trademarks of Simon & Schuster, Inc.
For information about special discounts for bulk purchases, please contact
Simon & Schuster Special Sales at 1-866-506-1949 or
business@simonandschuster.com.
Manufactured in the United States of America 0721 LAK
2 4 6 8 10 9 7 5 3 1
Library of Congress Cataloging-in-Publication Data
Names: Bauer, Marion Dane, author. | Wallace, John, 1966– illustrator.
Title: Mars / by Marion Dane Bauer ; [illustrated by] John Wallace.
Description: New York, New York : Simon Spotlight, 2021. | Series: Our
universe | Summary: "Explore the planet Mars in the second book in this
new, nonfiction Level 1 Ready-to-Read series about the universe that's
perfect for kids who love science and space!"— Provided by publisher.
Identifiers: LCCN 2021018768 | ISBN 9781534486454 (paperback) |
ISBN 9781534486461 (hardcover) | ISBN 9781534486478 (ebook) Subjects:
LCSH: Mars (Planet)—Juvenile literature. | Planets—Juvenile literature.
Classification: LCC QB641 .B38 2021 | DDC 523.43—dc23

Glossary

✦ **astronaut** (say: A-struh-not): a person who goes into outer space. We refer to astronauts as "cosmonauts" when they are from Russia, "spationauts" when they are from France, and "taikonauts" when they are from China.

✦ **gravity** (say: GRA-vuh-tee): a pulling force that works across space. The bigger an object is, the more pull it has.

✦ **microbes** (say: MY-krohbs): life-forms so small that we can't see them.

✦ **oxygen** (say: AHK-sih-jun): a colorless, odorless gas. About 21 percent of the atmosphere on Earth is oxygen. Most organisms on Earth need oxygen to breathe.

✦ **poisonous** (say: POY-zuhn-us): something that causes harm when it touches the skin or enters the body.

✦ **scientists** (say: SIE-uhn-tists): people who observe and do research or experiments in a particular area of interest to better understand the world around us.

✦ **solar system** (say: SOH-luhr SIH-stum): the sun together with the planets and their moons that orbit around it.

Note to readers: Some of these words may have more than one definition. The definitions above match how these words are used in this book.

Have you ever dreamed of visiting Mars?

Flying to Mars in a spaceship would take six months or more. It would be a journey filled with surprises.

Even from far away
you would see why Mars
is called the Red Planet.

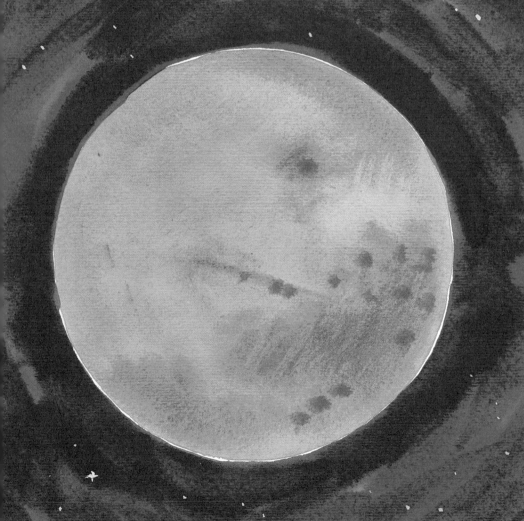

The red color comes
from iron dust in the air.

When you got to Mars,
our Sun would look small,
and the sky would be red.

But the sunset would
be blue.

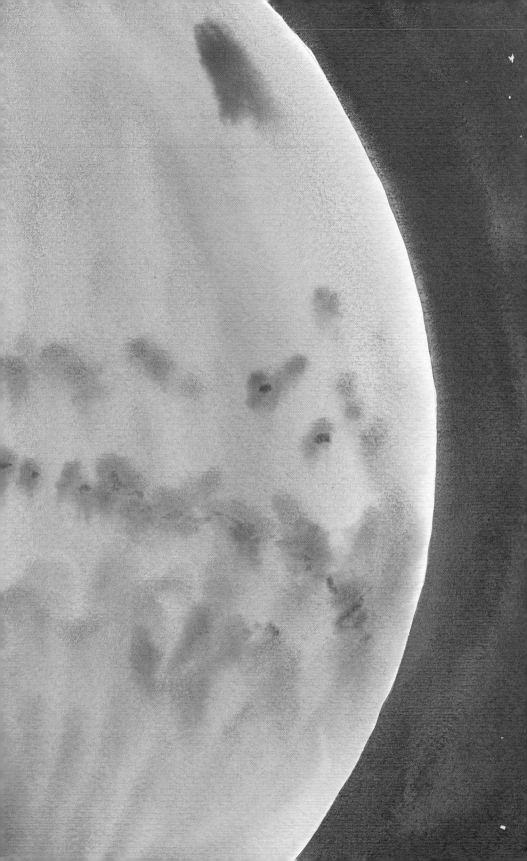

The night sky would
hold two moons.

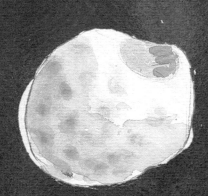

You could see the tallest
volcano in our **solar system**,
Olympus (say: uh-LIM-puhs)
Mons.

Olympus Mons is 374 miles wide. But it rises so gently that it is almost flat.

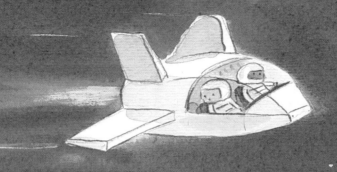

You could see the canyon
Valles Marineris
(say: VA-luhs ma-ruh-NAIR-is).

In some places, the huge
canyon is four miles deep.
It is as wide as the entire
United States.

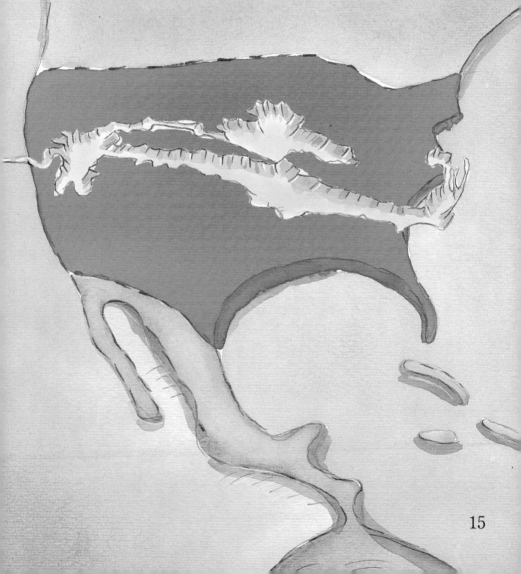

You could jump almost three times higher on Mars than you can on Earth.

That is because Mars has less surface **gravity** than Earth.

But do not pack your
bags yet!

Mars is a harsh planet.

Mars has very little **oxygen** and almost no water. Even the ground may be **poisonous**.

We need oxygen and water
to live.

And what about that wind?

Dust storms can last
for months!

Still, **scientists** love to study Mars.

They hope to find
signs of life there.

But they are looking
for **microbes,**

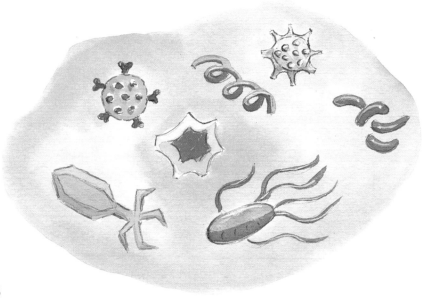

not aliens.

Many countries have sent spacecrafts to Mars.

Everyone wants to learn more about the Red Planet.

Maybe one day you will be the first **astronaut** to fly to Mars.

Or you might be a scientist
who discovers life there!

Interesting Facts

✦ Eight planets circle our Sun: Jupiter and Saturn are gas giants. Neptune and Uranus are ice giants. Mercury, Venus, Earth, and Mars are smaller and made of rock.

✦ Earth is the third planet from the Sun. Mars is the fourth.

✦ Mars is the planet most like ours. It is just a little more than half the size of Earth.

✦ The two moons of Mars are named Phobos and Deimos.

✦ Mars has frequent fierce storms. About once every three Martian years, a storm encircles the entire planet.

✦ The days on Mars are almost the same length as days on Earth, but the years are twice as long.

✦ The atmosphere on Mars is more than 95 percent carbon dioxide. Even the snow that falls near Mars's south pole is made of carbon dioxide.

✦ The average temperature of Mars is 80 degrees below zero Fahrenheit, and 63 degrees below zero Celsius.

✦ In 2021 the United States touched down on Mars. The parachute that gently lowered the space rover, *Perseverance*, to the surface had an orange-and-white design that carried the words "Dare Mighty Things" in code. The phrase is taken from a quote by former president Theodore Roosevelt.